O9-CFT-219

95-589

J
582.16
Plu

Pluckrose, Henry Arthur
Trees

DATE DUE			
SEP 1 9 1995			
MAR 1 3 1996			
JUL 2 0 2004			

Irene Ingle Public Library
P. O. Box 679
Wrangell, Alaska   99929

GAYLORD

WALKABOUT

Trees

Irene Ingle Public Library
P.O. Box 679
Wrangell, Alaska 9992c

Editor: **Ambreen Husain**
Design: **Volume One**

Photographs: Heather Angel—4, 28; Bruce Coleman
Ltd.—(G. Dore) 7, (F. Futil) 10, (P. Mortimer) 12,
(P. Clement) 15, (E. Pott) 17, (H. Reinhard) 20,
21, (B. Coleman) 20 inset, (E. Crichton) 21 inset,
(G. McCarthy) 25; Eye Ubiquitous—(K. Mullineaux)
16; Chris Fairclough Colour Library—14 inset, 23
insets, 29; Frank Lane Picture Agency—(Silvestris) 5,
(R. Wilmshurst) 9 inset, (E. & D. Hosking) 11,
(D. Robinson) 27; NHPA—(S. Dalton) 24, (E. A.
Janes) 31; Oxford Scientific Films—(H. Taylor)
cover, (K. & D. Dannen) 8, (G. A. Maclean) 22;
ZEFA—9, 13, 14, 15 inset, 23, 26

Additional photographs: Chris Fairclough

Library of Congress Cataloging-in-Publication Data

Pluckrose, Henry Arthur.
    Trees / by Henry Pluckrose.
       p.   cm. — (Walkabout)
    ISBN 0-516-08121-7
    1. Trees—Miscellanea—Juvenile literature.
[1. Trees.] I. Title. II. Series: Pluckrose, Henry
Arthur. Walkabout.
QK475.8.P58   1994
582.16—dc20   93-44699
                                                CIP
                                                AC

1994 Childrens Press® Edition
© 1993 Watts Books, London
All rights reserved. Printed in the United States of America.
Published simultaneously in Canada.
1 2 3 4 5 6 7 8 9 0 R 03 02 01 00 99 98 97 96 95 94

95-589 ✓

WALKABOUT
Trees

Henry Pluckrose

CHILDRENS PRESS ®

CHICAGO

Our wonderful world has
many kinds of plants.
There are grasses, flowers,
shrubs and bushes, and trees.

4

But what is special
about a tree?

5

Shrubs and bushes
have leaves, flowers,
and branches . . .
just like trees.
The branches of a
shrub grow straight
from the soil.

6

Now look at this tree.
A tree grows from one
single shoot . . . called
the trunk.
The branches grow
from the trunk.

The trunk and branches
of a tree are protected
by bark.
Bark keeps the tree cool
in summer and warm
in winter.
Bark keeps the tree from
being dried by the sun.

As the tree grows, the bark splits, cracks, and falls off.
There is always new bark underneath the old.

There are many kinds
of trees.
Each kind of tree has its
own special shape.
Some trees, like the English
oak, are tall and rounded.

Some, like the cedar, are shaped like a triangle.

11

Some droop . . . as
though they were sad,
like the lovely
weeping willow.

12

Some are straight and slim, like the poplar.

13

All trees have leaves.
Some trees keep their
leaves the year around.
These trees are called
evergreen trees.
In cold countries,
evergreens have spiky,
needle-shaped leaves.

14

Some trees lose their
leaves in the fall.
These are called
deciduous trees.
Most deciduous trees
have broad, flat leaves.

15

Leaves help make
the food trees need.
Roots carry water and
chemicals from the soil
to the branches and
the leaves.

Each leaf contains a green pigment called chlorophyll. The water and chemicals sucked up by the roots mix with the chlorophyll. When sunlight shines on them, the leaves make sugar.
Sugar is the food the tree needs to live.

You can identify trees
by the shape of their leaves.
Some leaves are triangle-shaped,
some are long and thin,
and some are quite feathery.
Which tree has a leaf
that is fan-shaped?

Mountain
Ash

Beech

Oak

Holly

Birch

Maple

Hawthorn

Chestnut

Willow

Alder

In springtime, many trees have flowers.

20

Without the flowers, there could be no fruit.

21

Inside each fruit
there are seeds.
A new tree could grow
from each of
these seeds!

These foods all grew on trees. Do you recognize any of them?

Many kinds of living creatures make their homes in trees. Animals often live around tree roots.

IRENE INGLE PUBLIC LIBRARY

Insects live beneath the bark . . . and provide food for birds.

High above the ground, squirrels are safe from their enemies.

Birds build their nests in holes in tree trunks and in the forks of branches.

When a tree is cut down,
you can see the pattern of
rings in the trunk.
It takes one year for each
ring to form.

28

When the small branches
have been cut from the
tree, the trunk is cut
into planks.

Wood is used for
many things . . .
for building houses,
for making furniture,
tools, toys, boxes . . .
and even paper.
Can you think of
other things that
wood is used for?

30

Would you like to live in a world without trees?

31

Index

About this book

Young children acquire information in a casual, almost random fashion. Indeed, they learn just by being alive! The books in this series complement the way young children learn. Through photographs and a simple text the readers are encouraged to comment on the world around them.

To a young child, the world is new and almost everything in it is interesting. But interest alone is not enough. If a child is to grow intellectually this interest has to be directed and extended. This book uses a well-tried and successful method of achieving this goal. By focusing on a particular topic, it invites the reader first to look and then to question. The words and photographs provide a starting point for discussion.

Children enjoy information books just as much as stories and poetry. For those who are not yet able to read print, this book provides pictures that encourage talk and visual discrimination—a vital part of the learning process.

Henry Pluckrose